office
OLYMPICS

OFFICE OLYMPICS

Text by Sarah Herman

Chapter icons by Andrew Li

Summersdale Publishers Ltd
46 West Street
Chichester
West Sussex
PO19 1RP
UK

www.summersdale.com

Printed and bound in Great Britain

ISBN: 978-1-84953-180-1

Substantial discounts on bulk quantities of Summersdale books are available to corporations, professional associations and other organisations. For details contact Summersdale Publishers by telephone: +44 (0) 1243 771107, fax: +44 (0) 1243 786300 or email: nicky@summersdale.com.

office
OLYMPICS

Tom Hay

summersdale

CONTENTS

INTRODUCTION

Step up to the mark, office athletes – your time to shine has finally come; your place of work just won the bid for the first Office Olympics and the competition starts right here, right now.

Whether you're a runner, a jumper, a swimmer, a gymnast, a horseback rider or a damn fine spectator, there's something in here to get your heart pumping. Test your throwing arm and get caffeinated in Java-lin; feel wet, wild and oh-so-minty in Water Polos or turn the conference room into a place where something fun happens for a change with Blu-tackle Hockey.

Office Olympics is the ideal way to inject a bit of healthy competition and bags of energy into your office without having to sacrifice those late-night curries, and you get to experience the spectacle without wearing running shorts, getting sweaty or spraining your ankle in an unfortunate hurdling heat.

Now, stride out into the stadium (show up to work), fire up the Olympic torch (turn the lights on) and let the games commence...

NB: The Office Olympics Committee holds no responsibility for any injuries, accidents or disciplinary action that may result directly or indirectly from participating in these events. All players take part at their own risk and should try to avoid breaking any bones or office furniture.

OPENING CEREMONIES

No Olympics would be complete without some grand show-stopping drama to kick things off. Get your muscle-pumping proceedings going with these ceremonious starters.

Welcome to Work

Two or more players required (the more the merrier!)

Apparatus:

- A5 paper (1 sheet per player)
- Colouring pens
- Dice
- Pencils (1 per player)
- Sticky tape
- Whistles (1 per player)

Warm-up:

Make a flag to show your support. Draw and colour your own creative flag design on a piece of paper. Alternatively, use the photocopier to enlarge one of the stock designs (see overleaf) and colour it in yourself. Using sticky tape, fix a pencil onto one side of the paper to make a flag.

How to Play:

Consider your office door as the entrance tunnel to the stadium. Each time someone walks through it it's up to players to welcome them to the Olympics in the proper manner. First, decide the order in which players will perform their greeting; then decide the type of greeting players will perform and the points they will earn by asking them each to roll the dice (see scoring list below). Players must then perform their assigned greeting for the next person who enters the room. If they choose to forfeit they win no points for that round.

Scoring:

If you roll:

1 – Wave your flag (score 1 point)

2 – Clap enthusiastically (score 2 points)

3 – Make a whooping sound (score 3 points)

4 – Shout, 'Team [your team name]!' repeatedly (score 4 points)

5 – Blow whistle and clap furiously (score 5 points)

6 – Sing the British national anthem and wave your flag (score 6 points)

Go for Gold:

Want to take things to the next level? Select a member of the office who's not playing (perhaps the boss) and whenever they walk in the room, no matter whose turn it is, every player must perform their last greeting in unison!

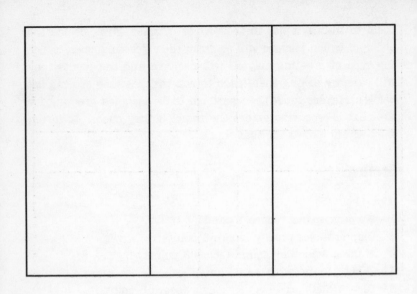

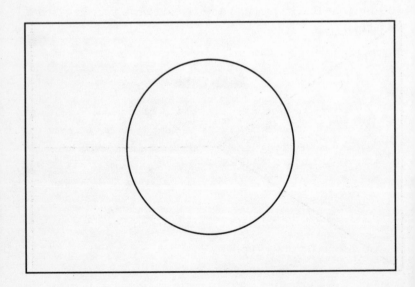

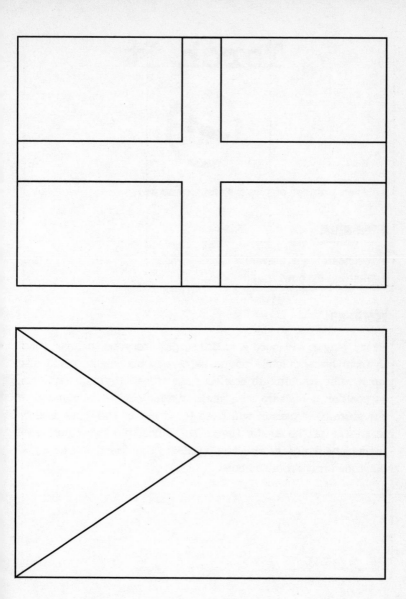

Torch It

An even number of players (four or more)

Apparatus:

- Torches (1 per player)
- Washing-up bowl

Warm-up:

Every player will need a torch, so get everyone to bring them in from home (mobile phone lights and bike lights could also work). The washing-up bowl is your office's Olympic cauldron, so position it high up on a shelf or filing cabinet at one end of the room. One person will need to sit out of the game and be in charge of the lights. Divide the office into two equal-sized teams, ensuring – as much as possible – that teams are an equal distance away from the bowl.

How to Play:

At any point during the day the person in charge of the lights can flip the light switch in the office, plunging all the players into (relative) darkness. As soon as this happens all the players must grab their torches and turn them on. The player from each team who is sitting furthest from the cauldron must run with their torch and put it in the bowl. When they've returned to their seat the next furthest player does the same, and so on until all team members have put their torches in the cauldron. Whichever team deposits all their torches the fastest is the winner.

Going for Gold:

If you lose to the other team, don't give up so easily. Make the event a 'best of three' or 'best of five' competition so you'll have a chance to win your pride back.

International Dance Party

Five or more players (plus one adjudicator)

Apparatus:

- A party music CD (or use an Internet radio station)
- Pen
- Sticky labels (as many as there are desks in the office)

Warm-up:

The adjudicator must prepare for the game by writing a different country on each sticky label and affixing one to each desk in the office. It's best to be discreet about this or to do the prep work while everyone is out on their lunch breaks.

How to Play:

An Olympics opening ceremony wouldn't be complete without some party music and a lot of dancing. To begin the game the adjudicator turns on the CD or radio station on their computer's speakers and all the participating players must dance around the office – they can carry on with their work but must be moving to the music. When the music stops the adjudicator shouts out the name of one of the countries they wrote on the labels and immediately all players must locate the desk with that country on it and touch the desk. Whoever is last to reach the desk (according to the adjudicator) is out. The music is then turned back on and the game continues. The winner is the last player left in at the end.

ATHLETICS

The crowd, the lights, the buzz of competition hanging in the air... feel the power of the athletics arena from the comfort of your swivel chair and learn what it means to be a champion with these modified versions of some ancient Greek classics.

Give Them the Run Around

Four or more players

Apparatus:

....

• Office phones (1 for each player)

How to Play:

....

Challenge one of your fellow workers to a sprint-off. Dial their extension and when they answer the phone pronounce yourself as the challenger and shout, 'Take your marks!' and then hang up. This lets the other player know that you've chosen them to compete against. Each player must then run as fast as they can to their opponent's desk and back to their own. Whoever makes it back and sits down at their desk chair first is the winner. The losing player can cool off in the kitchen where they must make tea for the victor. If the winner is too close to call, the decision is thrown open to the rest of the office who vote on who they think sat down first.

Scoring:

While it's not necessary to keep score by tallying up each player's wins, an overall sprint champion can be selected at the end of the week. As a sportsmanlike gesture they can get the first round at the pub on Friday.

Go for Gold:

Think you could give Usain Bolt a run for his money? Prove your zippy skills by upping the challenge. When your opponent picks up the phone shout to them the name of a different location they have to run to such as: 'the top floor', 'conference room' or 'the cafe across the road', then run your socks off to get there and back before they do.

Tea Break Trial

Quick games for busy people

One-minute Marathon

Two players (plus one adjudicator)

Apparatus:

• Stopwatch

How to Play:

Marathon running is all about pacing yourself. For this game both players remove their watches and stand in the centre of the office with their backs to each other. They have one minute (timed by the adjudicator) to touch the wall they're facing without turning around, but the winner is the *last* player to do so in the time limit. The game tests the players' ability to judge their opponent's nerve and the time. Whoever touches the wall last, without taking longer than a minute to do it, is the winner.

Walkabout

Two or more players (plus one adjudicator)

Apparatus:

- Piece of tape or ribbon
- Plastic recycling boxes (2 per player)

Warm-up:

Empty out the contents of the recycling boxes (be sure to recycle it all later!). All players are given two boxes, and stand with one foot in each. If your office does not have a central island of desks, or a central point, create one by moving furniture so there is a clear pathway around the perimeter of the office.

How to Play:

Line all the players up at the start line. When the adjudicator starts the race players must make their way around the central island (or central point) and back to the start line wearing the boxes on their feet. No running is allowed – although it's unlikely this will be possible – so the race is fairly slow. If a player crouches, falls or touches the floor or walls with their hands they are immediately disqualified from the race. The first player to make it to the finish line i.e. the start line with a piece of tape or ribbon held up by some helpful colleagues, with both their recycling boxes still on their feet, is the winner.

Going for Gold:

Although you're not allowed to touch the floor or walls with your hands, there's nothing to stop you making sure the other players break the rules. In Walkabout a small amount of competitive boisterousness is deemed appropriate. Nudge your fellow contestants, tickle them or knock their boxes with yours to give yourself an advantage. Don't get a reputation as being a trickster, though, as you'll have an entire gang of angry recycling boxes charging straight at you!

Curdles

Two or more players

Apparatus:

- 1-pint plastic bottles of milk (1 for each player)
- 10 boxes of copy paper

Warm-up:

Set up a small hurdling course from one end of the office to the other using the boxes of copy paper. Stack two boxes on top of each other to form one hurdle and repeat four times throughout the office to make five hurdles. Hand out the bottles of milk and remove the lids in preparation for the race.

How to Play:

Players take it in turns to run the five-hurdle course while holding an open carton of milk. Despite the low height of the hurdles, players must not simply step over the hurdle or step on it but are required to hop or jump over it, so both feet are off the ground at some point during the jump. Players can do the course as quickly or slowly as they choose. The aim is to keep the milk in the carton and not spill any on yourself (or your new office carpets).

Scoring:

The player with the most milk left in their carton is the winner. The player with the least amount of milk left must clean up the mess everyone else has made (now there's an incentive to be the best 'curdler' you can!).

Going for Gold:

Think hopping over the hurdles is too easy? Stack them one or even two paper boxes higher and see if you're gold medal material then!

USB-lays

An even number of players (six or more)

Apparatus:

- 2 USB memory sticks
- Computers (1 for each player)

Warm-up:

Divide the office up into two teams. Find an image online that best represents each team and save it onto the team's USB memory stick.

How to Play:

When the race starts the first player in each team takes the USB stick and loads their team's picture onto their computer and sets it as their desktop background. They must then eject the USB stick and throw it to another player in their team, who repeats the process. The winning team is the first team to have their image set as the desktop background on all of their computers. Any player that fails to catch the USB stick when it is thrown to them can pick up the USB from the floor but must restart their computer as a time penalty.

Going for Gold:

Prove your ability to USB-lay with the best of 'em with this game-changer. Rather than using a picture found online, the first player takes a photo of themselves using a digital camera or camera phone, transfers it onto the USB stick which they throw to the next player for the photo to be uploaded on their computer. They must then take a photo of themselves for the next player to upload, and so on. When the last player in your team has taken a photo of themselves they must run back to the first player and deliver the USB stick for the final picture to be uploaded.

Long Jump Silver

Two or more players

Apparatus:

- 2 fifty-pence pieces
- 5 twenty-pence pieces
- 10 ten-pence pieces
- 20 five-pence pieces
- Empty box
- Sticky tape
- Stopwatch

Warm-up:

Set up an empty box (or other large container) at one end of the office. Mark a line with the sticky tape on the floor at the other end of the room.

How to Play:

With four quid up for grabs, this game could make you rich (or at least give you enough spare change to pick up a chocolate bar on your lunch break) so it's worth getting involved. One at a time players jump from the marked line of tape towards the box or container, holding all of the silver in their hands. Any coins that drop when they jump are out of play. From their landing spot they have 15 seconds, timed by the other players, to throw as much change into the bowl as possible, one coin at a time. Obviously, the closer they have jumped the easier this should be. At the end of the time the amount of money in the bowl is added up to give that person their score. After all the players have jumped and thrown, the person who collected the most money in the bowl is the winner and gets to keep all of the silver for themselves.

Tea Break Trial

Quick games for busy people

Tipple Jump

Two players

How to Play:

Can't decide whose turn it is to make the tea? Let the tipple-jump test decide. The two people in disagreement stand next to each other on one side of the office. They must hop one step forward on one leg, hop the next step on the other leg and finally jump a third step with both legs together. Whoever makes it furthest across the room is the victor and the other player must make the tea.

High-five Jump

Two or more players

Apparatus:

- Blu-tack
- Paper
- Photocopier
- Ruler

Warm-up:

Photocopy your hand onto a piece of paper. If a photocopier isn't available you can always print a picture of a hand shape, or draw one yourself. Stick the piece of paper onto the wall using the Blu-tack next to a frequently used doorway about 1.8 m (6 ft) from the ground. Make sure it's a door everyone uses.

How to Play:

Every time anyone from the office walks out through the door, they must high-five the hand on the piece of paper. For those unfamiliar with the art of the high-five please consult the diagram opposite. Each hour someone must raise the piece of paper by 10 cm, using the ruler. As the hand moves further up the wall, it will become necessary for players to jump if they are to successfully high-five it. Only one attempt to reach the hand is allowed i.e. you cannot jump twice. If you fail to high-five (either you forget, you're too embarrassed or it's out of your reach) then you are immediately disqualified. During the final half-hour of the working day, any players still left in the competition must go head-to-head. Gather everyone round and raise the hand 10 cm at a time, having each player high-five jump until one person is declared the champion.

Going for Gold:

Make everyone work that little bit harder by posting a high-five hand on each side of the doorway to double the jumping madness.

Catavault
Conference

Four players

Apparatus:

- 2 boxes of paperclips
- 2 empty boxes
- 2 rulers

Warm-up:

Sneak off to a meeting room where there's a big table for this one. Clear away any chairs to make room at the far ends of the table.

How to Play:

One person in each team will be the catavaulter and the other the catcher. The two catchers stand holding a box each at one end of the large table while the two catavaulters stand in the opposite two corners of the room where the boxes of paperclips are, facing their partners. When the game begins they load up their rulers with one paperclip and run holding the ruler towards the desk, trying not to drop the paperclip. If they do drop it, they must return to their corner and begin again. When they reach the table, paperclip still loaded, they must catapult the paperclip towards their partner who has to try and catch it in the box. They then run back to their corners to get another paperclip. The game lasts for five minutes and the team with the most paperclips in their box at the end is the winner.

Disco Discus

Four or more players (plus one adjudicator)

Apparatus:

- Large roll of sticky tape (1 per player)
- Mobile phones (1 per player)

Warm-up:

Most people in the office only throw serious dance shapes when they're drunk at the Christmas party, but this game will have them up and dancing at any time of the day. To prepare for the Disco Discus:

- Hand out a roll of tape to each member of the office.

- One person should be appointed adjudicator and is given a list of the phone numbers of each competing player.

- Each player must change their mobile phone ringtone to an upbeat dance number.

How to Play:

The adjudicator calls the phone of any player at any time. When they hear their ringtone go off, no matter what they're doing, the player has 10 seconds to locate their roll of tape and dance for the office to the beat of the ringtone. When the phone goes to voicemail the adjudicator will hang up, and the player must slide the roll of tape along the floor as part of their final dance move, ending their turn. If a player fails to take their turn in time, they are immediately disqualified from the game. At the end of the day all the non-disqualified players gather outside in the car park for a final Disco Discus throw to determine the winner. The player who throws their roll of tape the furthest takes the crown.

Java-lin

Four or more players

Apparatus:

- Coffee mugs (1 per player)
- Pens (1 per player)
- Pot of freshly brewed coffee

Warm-up:

Office mornings can be tough stuff and there's nothing like a good cup of java to perk up your fellow workers. Brew a pot of aromatic coffee and let the smell waft into the office. Line up the mugs at different distances from one wall of the room (check the diagram for specifics).

How to Play:

Draw straws or use some other method to determine a random order of play. Each player will need a pen with the lid on. The game is simple: standing at a predetermined distance from the nearest mug – about 6 m ought to do the trick – each player has one chance to throw their pen java-lin. The aim is to get a pen into a mug, which is then out of play to other players. If they fail to hit a cup then they'll have to face the day caffeine-free. At the end of play any player who has successfully thrown a pen into a mug can then fill it up with some coffee.

Scoring:

The closest mugs are the easiest to aim for, so the first players will probably go for these, but any player who manages to get their java-lin in the mug closest to the wall automatically disqualifies all the other players and can claim the whole pot of coffee for themselves. If anyone gets their java-lin to land in a cup, then it's mandatory that they get a bonus biscuit too.

Tea Break Trial

Quick games for busy people

Shot-Foot

Two or more players

How to Play:

Soak up some fresh air on a 'cigarette break' by heading out into the car park to play this beauty. Players take it in turns to remove one shoe and stand at an agreed starting point. Shoe in hand they must rest it by their ear and launch it – shot-put style – as far as they can, without putting their shoeless foot on the ground until after their shoe has landed (otherwise this will lead to automatic disqualification). All shoes are left on the ground until all players have thrown. The winner is the shot-footer whose shoe goes the furthest.

Hammer and Cheese

Four players

Apparatus:

- 2 loaves of bread
- 2 packets of cheese squares
- 2 packets of ham slices
- 4 disposable plates

Warm-up:

This popular spectator game requires two teams of two and an enthusiastic crowd. Take your lunch outside and set up two sandwich-making stations with a loaf of bread, packet of cheese, packet of ham and two plates at each station.

How to Play:

At the whistle both teams have three minutes to make as many ham and cheese sandwiches as possible and catch the contents on a plate. One player makes the sandwich, spins in a circle three times and hurls the sandwich towards their teammate who must try and catch it on one of the plates. Once caught, they can turn the contents of their catch onto their second plate and prepare to catch the next sandwich. The winner is the team who accumulates the most points at the end of the time limit.

Scoring:

Points will be awarded for the following:

- Per slice of bread: 2 points
- Per square of cheese: 2 points
- Per slice of ham: 2 points

Hardcore Hep Hop

Two or more players (plus one adjudicator at the finish line)

Apparatus:

• Blu-tack
• Paper (1 sheet per player)
• Pencils (1 per player)
• Teabags (1 per player)

How to Play:

This game is all about speed, jumping like a crazy gazelle and exerting a tiny amount of physical strength. Because it's quite disruptive to the office, it's probably a good idea to wait until people's eyes are glazing over around five o'clock and then start playing. When the game begins all players must:

• Sprint the length of the office four times.

• Bunny-hop the length of the office four times (jumping with both feet together).

• Throw a tea bag (unused) down the length of the office – you must throw it again from wherever it lands until you reach the end.

- Draw a quick sketch of your boss.

- Run with that sketch and, using Blu-tack, stick it above the office doorway.

- Scramble over three desks.

- Run from wherever you end up after desk-scrambling to reception (or the office front door if you don't have a reception) to receive your place on the leader board.

Whoever makes it to reception first is the winner.

Scoring:

Allocate each player the same number of points as the position that they came (e.g. if you came first you get one point, second receives two points, etc.) Play the game once a week for seven weeks in a row – perhaps as a fun way to end things on a Friday. After seven weeks, add up everyone's points. The player with the least points is the overall Hardcore Hep Hop champion.

WATER SPORTS

Don't panic! There's still no chance of seeing your boss in Speedos (unless he's into *very* casual Fridays), just lots of good, clean, slightly damp fun.

Shoe Canoe Slalom

Two or more players

Apparatus:

- 10 coffee mugs
- Masking tape
- Shoes (1 per player)
- Small bottle of water
- Stopwatch

Warm-up:

Mark a starting line and a finishing line at opposite ends of the office using masking tape. In between the two lines place the coffee mugs next to each other in pairs to make five 'gates'. Place each pair about 20 cm apart and equally space the gates from each other. The gates should not be in a line and should zigzag down the room. See the handy little diagram opposite. Each player must remove one shoe and line up to take their turn at the slalom run.

How to Play:

To claim the gold medal for your own, you need to put the bottle of water in your shoe and move your shoe, using only your shoeless foot from start to finish. You must slide the shoe by pushing it or kicking it (not putting your foot back in the shoe). The shoe must be manoeuvred through each mug gate without touching the sides. Penalties will be incurred for mug-touching. If the water bottle falls out of the shoe, you must return to the start line and begin again, you fool.

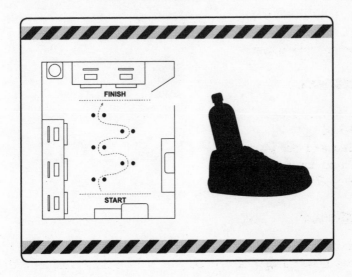

Scoring:

This game is not all about speed. For every time you touch a mug you will incur a ten-second penalty, i.e. ten seconds will be added to your time. The player with the fastest time after all penalties are considered is the winner.

Tea Break Trial

Quick games for busy people

Different Folks, Different Strokes

Three players

How to Play:

Draw straws to decide which player gets each of these three swimming strokes (front crawl, breast stroke and butterfly). Whenever a player leaves the office e.g. to go to a meeting, the kitchen or the toilet they must walk performing their stroke with their arms. One point is awarded for each successful stroke exit. Two points are awarded to any player who leaves the room walking backwards performing back stroke. The player who has the most points at the end of the day wins the gold.

Skiving Diving

Two players (plus one adjudicator)

Apparatus:

- Bowl of water (if you don't have any bowls in the office, use a plastic recycling box or Tupperware box)
- Eraser
- Plastic ruler
- Sticky tape

Warm-up:

Find a willing opponent who sits near you and tape a flexible plastic ruler to the end of your desk. Fill up a bowl with water and position it on the floor just ahead of where the end of the ruler finishes. The handy diagram will show you the physics of the whole shebang.

How to Play:

Take it in turns to show off your aerial moves by placing an eraser on the end of the ruler nearest to the bowl and with one finger pull down on the ruler's edge and let go to propel the eraser into the air and (hopefully) down into the bowl. The crowd goes wild! A third chum should act as an independent adjudicator, judging the dives out of ten for the following criteria: accuracy, height and flair.

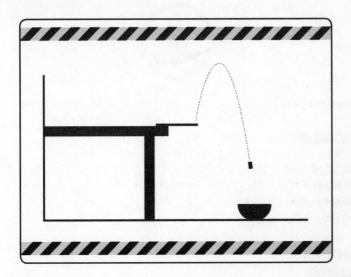

Scoring:

Points are awarded accordingly:

- Accuracy: in the bowl (10 points); within the close vicinity of the bowl (5 points); pretty far from the bowl (1 point); can't find it? (0 points)

- Height: really high (10 points); a good attempt (5 points); it hopped (1 point); it just fell off the ruler. (0 points)

- Flair: wow! What is that? (10 points); Yep, you know your stuff, eraser (5 points); Seen it before (1 point); You did nothing. NOTHING. (0 points)

I Am Sailing

Three players

Apparatus:

- 3 desk fans
- A4 paper
- Conference-sized table
- Sugar cubes

Warm-up:

Ahoy there budding sailors! Think you've got what it takes to take on the mighty winds of your open-plan office? (And we're not talking about the gale-force flatulence after you boss ate a dodgy curry.) First each of the three players must build a suitable vessel. Each sailor is allowed to use one sheet of A4 paper to build a craft of some sort. The only requirement is that it can hold one cube of sugar.

How to Play:

When all the cubes of sugar are aboard their paper boats, move the action to the conference room (or another large desk in the office). At one end of the table position the three desk fans with one boat lined up in front of each. When the fans are switched on the race commences. The boat that travels the furthest down the table without losing its sugar cube is the winner.

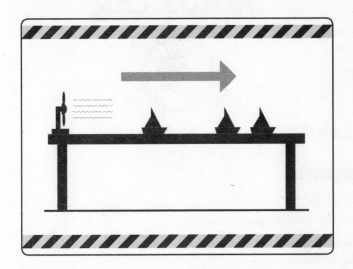

Synchronised Snacking

An even number of players (four or more)

Apparatus:

- Satsuma or small orange equivalent (one per team)
- Swivel chairs (two per team)

Warm-up:

If there's one sure-fire way to get the office motivated for some Olympic fun it's a healthy snack. Divide the office up into teams of two and give each team a satsuma or other small orange. They must peel the orange before the game starts. Make sure all satsumas in play have the same number of segments.

How to Play:

At the start of play all teams must be sitting near to each other in their swivel chairs and next to a desk. One member of the team begins holding the orange. The aim of the game is to eat your team's orange in the fastest time while incorporating some swivel moves. To begin, and without their bodies touching the floor, teams must push off from their desk, manoeuvre around each other, hand over the orange, and return to their desks. Once the orange has been handed over, the player holding it must eat a segment. This process is repeated until all the segments have been eaten. The winning team is the first one to eat their whole fruit and return to their desks.

Going for Gold:

Incorporating these synchronised swivel moves is tough, but if it's not tough enough for you then you can always add in this rule: teammates cannot touch each other or each other's chairs during the competition. With no assistance from your partner you will have to brush up on your swivel skills if you want to win.

Row, Row, Row Your Boss

An even number of players (four or more)

Apparatus:

- Cardboard box large enough for a person to crouch or sit in
- Stopwatch

Warm-up:

If you're the boss this is a great one to get the folks in your office motivated. You may not be David Brent but that doesn't mean you can't have fun. Rally the troops and set some kind of prize for winning the game – drinks on you after work, perhaps? If you're not the boss, then you're going to need them on board for this one (literally), so pick a day when they're feeling happy and ask them to come and take part.

How to Play:

Divide the room into groups of two. The office boss must climb inside the open cardboard box and sit down. With one team member pulling from the front, and one pushing from the back, the team must move the boss across the floor to two designated pit stops along the route, and back to the starting point (see the diagram for possible pit stops). The team must also sing, in unison, 'Row, row, row your boss/gently on the floor/merrily, merrily, merrily, merrily/working here's a bore!' to the melody of 'Row, Row, Row Your Boat', continuously around the course. The team to get the boss back to home base in the fastest time shall be victorious. Teams who fail to reach the pit stops or are not singing enthusiastically, can be eliminated at the boss's discretion.

Going for Gold:

Finding dragging your boss around the room while singing not much of a challenge? Get your boss to load up the box with extra weight at each pit stop. Perhaps with a couple of reams of paper on board the whole thing won't be such a breeze.

Tea Break Trial

Quick games for busy people

Car Park
Water Polo

Two players

Apparatus:

- 2 buckets/plastic boxes half full of water
- 2 cups

How to Play:

Outside, away from electrical wiring and expensive office equipment, set up the two buckets at opposite ends of the car park. Starting beside their own buckets with a cup players must run to their opponent's bucket and using their cup they must carry as much water back to their own bucket as possible (one cupful at a time) trying not to spill it. After five minutes of play, the player with the most water left in their bucket is the winner. For a more frenzied version make this into a team game.

BATS AND BALLS

Hand–eye coordination, fancy footwork and ball skills will all come into play over the next few pages. But if you're a bit crap at all of the above you'll still have a jolly good time. Just watch out for flying objects!

Padminton

Two players (plus one adjudicator to keep score)

Apparatus:

- 2 mouse mats
- Large eraser
- Sticky tape
- Tissue

Warm-up:

Now's your chance to show off those shuttlecock skills. First you'll need to make the shuttlecock as they can be hard to come by in the office. Wrap a large eraser in a tissue and use some sticky tape to secure it.

How to Play:

As it's unlikely anyone will bother to bring a full-sized badminton net to work, there is no need for one in Padminton, but if you have desk partitions in your office, make the most of these. Just find a trustworthy adjudicator, pick your opponent, seize your mouse mat and stand on opposite sides of the desk. Take it in turns to serve the 'shuttlecock' over the desk. You only have one shot to get the shuttlecock over the desk, if you fail, service switches to the other player. After a player has served (for which no points are scored), every time either player successfully hits the shuttlecock back over the desk they score one point. If it hits the floor, lands on the desk or does not make it over the desk then the turn ends and the other player starts to serve. To win the game you need to score more points than your opponent, so it's important to keep the rally going. The game lasts for five services each, after which it's time to add up the scores and prove who could really cut it with the big boys.

Scoring:

• 1 point is scored for each successful rally hit (not counting the service hits)

• 2 points are awarded for a hit that a player cannot return

Basket Case

An even number of players (six or more)

Apparatus:

- 2 small waste-paper bins
- Newspaper
- Sticky tape
- Swivel chairs

Warm-up:

Put a waste-paper bin at each end of the room and divide the office up into two teams, making sure people from each team are seated all over the office. Scrunch up a few sheets from the newspaper and secure it into a ball shape using the tape. Game time!

How to Play:

Each team has a 'home bin', which they must protect from being reached by the other team while trying to score in the opposing team's bin. Players must remain seated throughout play and begin each round at their desk. A coin toss determines which team has the ball first. A player in the centre of the office begins with the ball. When you are holding the ball you cannot move your chair across the floor (only stationary swivelling is allowed). Players must pass the ball to their teammates in an attempt to score a basket in the other team's bin. Whichever team doesn't have possession must try and get the ball by intercepting passes between the other team's players. One point is scored for each successful basket. The game lasts for four five-minute periods or until your boss appears to ask what all the racket is about. Good luck explaining that one.

Blu-tackle Hockey

An even number of players (six or more)

Apparatus:

- 2 desk trays
- 30-cm rulers (one for each player)
- Blu-tack
- Small rectangular erasers (one for each player)
- Tape

Warm-up:

Fashion a truly awesome Blu-tackle hockey stick by affixing the eraser to the bottom end of a ruler using the tape (see diagram). Create a Blu-tackle ball using a small hunk of Blu-tack so it's about the size of a table tennis ball and set up the two desk trays as goals at each end of a large table – perhaps in the conference room if you have one. Divide the group into two teams and appoint one player in each team as goalkeeper.

How to Play:

The aim is to get the ball into the opposing team's desk tray by tackling your opponents and passing to your teammates. One point is scored for each goal and the main rules to follow are:

- The last team to touch the ball before it is knocked off the table must pick up the ball, reshape it and hand it to the other team to take control from the centre of the table.

- It's important to tackle as much as possible to gain possession of the ball, but if during the tackle you flatten the ball you have to sit out for one minute.

- If your Blu-tackle stick breaks during play, you must withdraw from play until you have fixed your stick to a useable standard.

Tea Break Trial

Quick games for busy people

Hot Shot

Two or more players

Apparatus:

- 1 sheet of scrap A4 paper
- Waste-paper bin
- Sellotape or sticky notes

Scrunch up the piece of scrap paper to use as the ball (shared by all players) and place the empty waste-paper bin upright and away from the wall – rebound shots aren't allowed! Players must attempt to successfully throw the ball into the bin from a set distance, which should increase at intervals; as soon as a throw is missed the player is out and their distance is marked on the floor using some tape or a sticky note. The winner is the person who scores a successful throw from furthest away. If you're running out of floor space to increase the distance between the goal and the shooter, downsize the apparatus: use an A5 paper ball and a coffee mug for the goal – that should sort the hotshots from the peashooters.

Footsieball

An even number of players (six or more)

Apparatus:

- Newspaper
- Sticky tape
- Swivel chairs

Warm-up:

Make a ball using a few sheets of screwed-up newspaper balled together and secured using some tape. Divide the office into two teams, sit on your swivel chairs, and space the teams out down the length of the room.

How to Play:

The aim of Footsieball is to move the ball from one end of the chain of players to the other without letting it touch the ground and for the last player to kick the ball to the wall. The ball must be passed using feet only before a goal attempt is made (a typical Footsieball pass is shown in the diagram). Players are allowed to move their chairs, but they must stay seated throughout the game. Toss a coin to see which team starts with the ball first. If the ball drops onto the floor, possession is automatically passed to the nearest member of the opposing team. Tackles are allowed, but a tackle that causes the ball to fall to the floor will result in the ball being passed to the last person in the tackled team's chain.

Scoring:

When the last player in the chain has possession of the ball, they must toss the ball using their feet from the point they received it. If the ball hits the wall they score one point and can pick it up and throw it back to the start of their own line. If it doesn't, possession passes immediately to the closest player on the other team. The team with the most points after 20 minutes of play wins.

ACTION SPORTS

Want to take a swing at that new manager of yours? Take it to the parking lot, people. Want to prove your Olympic stature as a hole-punching, weight-lifting, thumb-wrestling champion? Read on...

Hole Punching

Two players

Apparatus:

- 2 blindfolds
- 2 hole punches
- Copy paper
- Photocopier

Warm-up:

Get ready for the punch of your life. Both players head to the photocopier and press their face against the glass to photocopy their best squished, punched face onto paper. The two players fold their piece of paper in half and exchange photocopies.

How to Play:

Blindfold each of the players and hand them their photocopy and hole punch. Using their hole punch, at the adjudicator's command, each player must punch out as many holes as possible in the photocopy of their opponent's face in one minute. They must try to avoid tearing the page or punching holes in any area of the page that is not covered by their opponent's face. After one minute the number of points for each player is totalled to reveal the hole-punching champion.

Scoring:

- 1 point will be awarded for each hole punched on the face of an opponent
- 1 point will be deducted for each hole not punched on the face of an opponent
- 2 points will be deducted for a tear to the page
- An extra 10 points will be awarded to any player who successfully punches out the centre of both their opponent's eyes

Tea Break Trial

Quick games for busy people

You Got Served

Two players

Apparatus:

• Ball of elastic bands

How to play:

You know that ball of elastic bands you've had sitting on your desk forever? Now is the chance to put it to good use. Play this game with the person who sits opposite you. Take it in turns to serve the ball volleyball-style using your palm, hitting it upwards towards the ceiling. The ball must hit your opponent's desk to score a point. Score two points if the ball lands on the desk. Take it in turns to serve. Whoever has the most points after five minutes is the winner.

NB: Don't have a ball of elastic bands? Try using an eraser or a stress ball.

Water Weight

Two or more players (plus one adjudicator)

Apparatus:

- 3 pairs of different sized bottles filled with water (suggested bottle size: 500 ml, 1 litre, 1.5 litres)
- Blackboard chalk
- Measuring jug (or use the kettle)
- Stopwatch

Warm-up:

Looking the part is an essential element to being a confident weightlifter. Crush up the blackboard chalk and insist all participating players dust their hands with it. Make sure all the bottles of water are full and position them in pairs of the same size from one side of the room to the other (from lightest at the start to heaviest at the end).

How to Play:

One player at a time takes to the floor to prove their weightlifting potential. Timed by an appointed adjudicator each player must shoulder press the two bottles of water at each station five times (see diagram) before drinking as much of ONE of the bottles of water as possible. Then they can move on to the following stations and repeat the process, drinking as much water as they can while trying to complete the course as quickly as possible.

Scoring:

After each player has finished, the amount of water left at each station in the three drinking bottles is combined and the total is added to the player's final time: ten seconds for every 100 ml remaining. The player with the fastest time is the winner.

Going for Gold:

Weightlifting is thirsty work, so why not jazz up Friday afternoon training by adding a little alcoholic flavour to these water weights to get everyone in the party spirit.

Taekwondoodle

Two or more players (plus one adjudicator)

Apparatus:

- Bag of party balloons
- Coloured marker pens
- Drawing pins

Warm-up:

Players are paired up with an opponent. Each player blows up a balloon and fixes it to the wall at waist height with a drawing pin. All players must be barefoot before the match commences. Appoint a trustworthy member of the office as the adjudicator.

How to Play:

Standing in front of their opponent's balloon, the players have one minute to:

- Draw two eyes, a nose, a mouth, two ears and hair onto the balloon using the marker pens.
- Kick the balloon ten times.

Scoring:

After the minute is up points will be awarded by the adjudicator accordingly:

- 2 points each for drawing eyes, nose, mouth, ears and/or hair
- 1 point for every kick completed in the time

The winner is the Taekwondoodler who scores the most points. If there are enough players organise the winners of each match to face off against each other in a knockout tournament.

Thumb Wrestling

Two players (plus one adjudicator)

Apparatus:

• Mouse mat

Warm-up:

This is a two-player game, but spectators are essential to the drama. Appoint someone to act as an adjudicator to keep score. This is Olympic-level thumb wrestling, so make sure you limber up before going into battle.

How to Play:

The mouse mat acts as the play arena. Both players, using their right hands, hold each other's hand as they would in a typical thumb wrestle (see diagram) on top of the mouse mat. Each match is comprised of three rounds and each round lasts for one minute. At the adjudicator's signal each player attempts to wrestle their opponent's thumb. Points are scored for specific moves and achievements as outlined opposite. The opponent with the most points at the end of the match is the Office Olympics Thumb Wrestling Champion.

Scoring:

The adjudicator awards 1 point for the following moves:

- Each time a player touches the nail of their opponent's thumb, with their thumb
- Each time a player forces their opponent's hand flat down on the mouse mat
- Each time a player causes their opponent to yelp with pain or frustration

The adjudicator awards 5 points (and ends the round) if either player pins down their opponent's thumb for more than five seconds.

Going for Gold:

Want to look the business on the wrestling mat? Decorate your thumb beforehand with coloured pens to really intimidate your opponent.

Foodo Judo

Two or more players

Apparatus:

• Lunch (bring your own)

Warm-up:

Foodo Judo is just like Judo only nobody gets grappled to the floor and forced to submit for fear of extreme pain. This game is ideal for rainy office lunch breaks. Wait till everyone has got their lunch out at their desks and let the games begin...

How to Play:

The reigning Foodo champion (or simply the person who wants to get the game started) challenges a player to a stare-off. Both players stare at each other until one blinks or looks away. The player who blinks or looks away is forced to submit and taps on their desk announcing they are out of the Foodo match and must hand over something from their lunch to the victor. The winner must then challenge another player, and so on. The game continues throughout the entire lunch break or until everyone has been challenged to a Foodo match.

Going for Gold:

Take this one to the pub for Friday lunchtimes and play for drinks or bar snacks. Watch out, though. If you're the Foodo Friday Champion you might be too tipsy to make your way back to the office. (Oh darn.)

ARMED AND DANGEROUS

There is never an appropriate time to bring your weapon of choice into work, so feel free to release your inner Robin Hood (or John McClane) by playing these games without a warrant being issued for your arrest.

Good Shot!

Ten players

Apparatus:

- 10 whiteboard magnets (5 of one colour and 5 of another)
- Whiteboard
- Whiteboard pens (black, blue, red)

Warm-up:

Set up the whiteboard at eye level and draw a circular target in the centre in black, about the circumference of a coffee mug. Around that draw another two larger circles; colour the first one red and the second one blue. See the handy diagram to make sure your target is up to Olympic standards.

How to Play:

Divide players into two teams of five and distribute the whiteboard magnets (one colour for team A and the other for team B) so that every player has one. Standing a desk length away from the whiteboard (mark this out on the floor with a piece of chalk, or some paper) teams take it in turns for players to throw their magnets, one player at a time, at the target.

There are two main throws used in this game – the 'scoop' (a basic underarm throw), which is used to try and secure the magnet onto the target or the 'smash' (an aggressive overarm throw) which players use to try and knock the other team's magnets out of play. Players must think tactically, as they only have five throws per round and should discuss as a team how best to proceed with each throw. Three rounds are played and the winning team is the one with the most points.

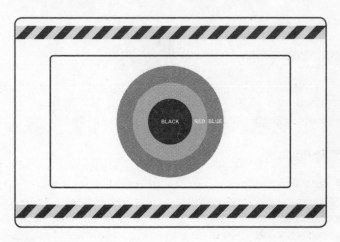

Scoring:

Points are awarded for any magnets that are on the board at the end of the match.

- 1 point for a magnet on the board but not on the target
- 2 points for a magnet on the blue circle
- 4 points for a magnet on the red circle
- 8 points for a magnet on the black circle

Tea Break Trial

Quick games for busy people

Fence Off

Two players

Apparatus:

• 2 pens

How to Play:

Challenge a colleague to a duel by approaching them, raising your pen and shouting 'En garde!'. Your opponent must then respond by raising their pen, and the fight commences. Players must hit their pens together throughout the fight unless they are lunging (trying to touch their partner's body with their pen) or trying to knock their opponent's pen from their hand. Score 1 point every time a player touches their opponent's body with their pen and 3 points if a pen is successfully knocked out of an opponent's hand. The game is over when a player is forced back to a wall or after one minute.

Archery For Dummies

Two or more players

Apparatus:

- Paper target (blow up the version printed in this book)
- Pencils (1 per player)

Warm-up:

Create a paper target on a piece of A4 paper. Save time by enlarging the handy version in this book on a photocopier. Stick it up on a wall near the door at an average shoulder height and hand out a sharpened pencil to all the players.

How to play:

On the way out of the office for Friday beers make everyone line up 2 m away from the target. One by one all players must aim their pencil at the target and launch it forward, attempting to make a mark on the paper. Whoever gets their makeshift arrow to make a mark closest to the centre is the winner and is exempt from buying a round at the bar.

Switch It Up:

Use this game to make all kinds of decisions in the office. The winner can be rewarded cups of tea, biscuits, new office stationery or equipment or can be exempt from tiresome duties such as cleaning the kitchen, doing the photocopying or attending meetings.

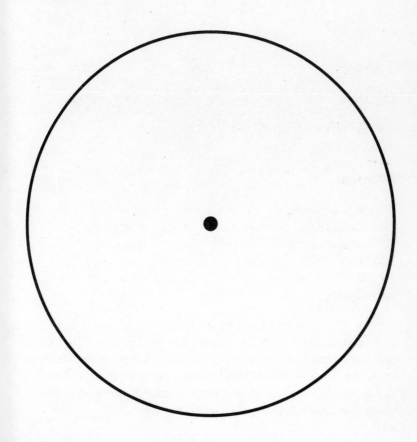

GYMNASTICS

Is bendy your middle name? Then you'll be sure to have some flexible fun with these gymnastics-inspired games. Be sure to limber up, but don't feel the need to wear a leotard to work. No one needs to see that.

I've Got Rhythm

Two or more players (plus three adjudicators)

Apparatus:

- 3 staplers
- Computer speakers
- Large cardboard box
- Large sheet of bubble wrap
- Packing tape
- Ruler

Warm-up:

Competing as a rhythmic gymnast at an international level takes years of dedication, so it's only fair that you put in a bit of craft time to prep the props required for this game.

- To make a hoop, cut a 10-cm section off the top of the cardboard box, taping the joins to make sure it's secure.

- Cut a long strip of bubble wrap from the sheet and tape it to the ruler to make a ribbon.

- To make the clubs (staplers) competition-ready they should be wrapped in bubble wrap and packing tape.

- Scrunch up the rest of the bubble wrap into a ball shape and secure it using the tape – this will serve as a ball.

How to Play:

This event tests your ability to interpret music using rhythmic gymnastics skills and props. Three adjudicators must score each player out of ten for their performance for an overall score out of 30. Using a classical music CD for the accompanying music, the adjudicators turn the speakers up and press play. The player must select a prop and perform around the office with it in time to the music. After ten seconds the adjudicators select the next track in the playlist, and the player must select another prop and adapt to the new music. The music is changed once more for a total performance time of around 30 seconds. After all of the players have performed the judges reveal the winner.

Desk Trampette

Two or more players (plus one adjudicator)

Apparatus:

- Box of large elastic bands
- Empty tissue box
- Small eraser

Warm-up:

Not all of us are lucky enough to have a full-sized Olympic trampoline in our offices (or the ceiling height to accommodate it); fortunately, the desk trampette means you can enjoy the bounce without even breaking into a sweat. First you have to build it. Loop elastic bands around the end of an empty tissue box and push them down to cover the opening. Make sure all the elastic bands are close to each other to create a springy surface (see diagram).

How to Play:

One person is required to hold the trampette and judge players. Trampetteers are invited up one at a time and are handed the eraser. They have three bounces with the eraser to demonstrate their physical and artistic trampette skills. They must accurately bounce the eraser on the trampette, catch it and then perform one of three regulation moves: a press-up, a cartwheel or a forward roll. They can perform any or all of the three moves in which order they choose and will be marked accordingly.

Scoring:

- 1 point is awarded for each accurate throw and catch of the eraser hitting the trampette (for a maximum of 3 points)
- Each press-up earns 10 points
- Each cartwheel earns 5 points
- Each forward roll earns 2 points

Tea Break Trial

Quick games for busy people

Floor Worker

Two players

How to Play:

This game will help prove you've got the gymnastic skills to wipe the floor with those teenage Russians. Two players must race from one side of the room to the other, performing the following sequence of moves: forward roll, cartwheel, 360-degree spin, star jump, forward roll. The player who makes it to the far side of the room first, having successfully completed all the moves is the winner.

CYCLING AND EQUESTRIAN

You may not be big on the whole green 'cycling to work' thing, but that doesn't mean you can't embrace your inner biker in the office. And as for the equine sports, well, they don't call you an old workhorse for nothing!

On Yer Bike

Four players

Apparatus:

- 4 different coloured marker pens
- Rolls of packing tape (1 per player)
- Staircase (2 flights where possible)

Warm-up:

Each player receives a roll of packing tape and a coloured marker. Before the race, each player should colour a cool mountain-bike-tastic design on the outside of their roll of tape to distinguish it from the other players' rolls.

How to Play:

All players begin the game at the top of two flights of stairs (see opposite for if you only have one flight at your office). When the race begins players must release their rolls of tape and watch from the top of the stairs as they hurtle down to the next floor. Only when their roll of tape stops moving can they follow it down the stairs and retrieve it. On picking up their tape they must jump on the spot ten times before sending it down the second flight. Again, when the tape stops moving they can run to the bottom of the 'mountain' and retrieve it before running back up to the top of both flights of stairs (watching out for other people's rolls that are still heading downwards!). The first player to reach the top with their tape is the winner. If your office only has one flight of stairs, after retrieving your tape from its first landing, run back up to the top of the stairs and let go from there for the second 'mountain' instead.

Tea Break Trial

Quick games for busy people

Bike-barrow Pursuit

Four players

How to Play:

Two teams of two line up at opposite ends of the office. One team member is the cyclist, the other is the bike. Players must assume the 'wheelbarrow race' position, and take their marks. Once the race is under way the two cyclists must steer their partner in a clockwise direction around the office with the goal of catching up with the other team. If they manage to 'tag' the other team by touching either teammate they win the round. Each round lasts for one minute – if neither team catch each other in the time then the round is a draw. Play best of three to decide the winning team.

Swivel Chair Dressage

Two or more players (plus one adjudicator)

Apparatus:

- Some ribbon
- Swivel chair
- Top hat (optional)

Warm-up:

You sit on your chair every day at work, so it's the closest thing you've got to a loyal steed. Decorate it with ribbons for its big performance and make sure all the wheels and joints are moving nicely. Appoint a member of the office to act as an adjudicator.

How to Play:

Don your top hat (if you happen to have one hanging around the office), mount your chair and push out into the arena (the middle of the office). You have two minutes to score as many points as possible, and you must complete the following tests during that time to avoid disqualification:

- Three pirouettes must be included in the performance – a pirouette requires you to swivel the chair 360 degrees on the spot.
- You must visit three of your fellow employees' desks and bow your heads to them before the two minutes is up.
- You must raise and lower the height of your chair at least once during the performance.

Scoring:

Points will be awarded out of ten in three categories to reveal a final score out of 30 for each participant. The rider with the highest overall score is the winner. The adjudicator must award points out of ten for the following categories:

- Chair decoration and individual flair
- Execution of the required components
- Originality of performance (paying close attention to the finish)

Leap Frog, Leap Horse

An even number of players (12 or more players)

Apparatus:

• Stopwatch

Warm-up:

Divide the office up into two teams and designate half of the office space to each team. Ideally you will have six or more players on each side.

How to Play:

Show those Olympic horses how to jump with style in this awesome team leap-frogging game. Each team lines up their players, spreading them evenly from one side of the room to the other. All players assume the leapfrog position except one player at the end of the line. When the claxon sounds (no claxon is necessary, someone can just shout, 'Go!') the standing player must leapfrog their way to the other end of the line, whinnying as they go. When they reach the end, they assume the leapfrog position, everyone shuffles down, and the next player follows them down the line. This repeats until the first player is back at the end of the line, at which point the whole team must run back to their office chairs. When everyone is seated, they can declare themselves the 'whinnyers'!

Going for Gold:

Want to make more of the course and show your horsey prowess? Rather than just leapfrogging, crawl through the legs of every other player. And sneak a bucket of water in front of one position on the course which you have to avoid, or risk getting very wet.

Tiny Team Triathlon

An even number of players (six or more)

Apparatus:

- 2 buckets of water
- 4 large toilet rolls

Warm-up:

When there's a lot of important reports to write and sales to make there just isn't time in the day to swim, cycle and run around like an Olympian. Never fear – this mini version will leave you feeling pumped, invigorated and ready for some more filing (whoop!). Take this one out to the car park to save any unnecessary spillages. Place the two buckets of water at one end of the car park, with two large rolls of toilet paper next to each one. Divide the players into two teams and line each team up behind a bucket.

How to Play:

When the race starts, one member of each team must dunk their face in the bucket of water and perform four front crawl strokes with their arms while submerged. Then, after taking their heads out of the water, they must push the two toilet rolls simultaneously, one hand on each, to the other end of the car park (see diagram). Dropping the toilet rolls, they must then run back to their team as fast as they can, handing over to the next player who dunks their head, performs four strokes, runs to the far end of the car park and rolls the toilet rolls in the same way back to the start line. When all members of the team have completed the course they must sit on the floor to prove their victory. The winning team is the first with all their players safely home with their bottoms on the floor.

Switch It Up:

Are the office cleaners getting annoyed that you keep stealing all the toilet rolls? Rather than push toilet rolls around, sit on a swivel chair and have the next person in the line push you to send you flying down the course.

MEDALS

Remember when you were in the sack race at school and didn't get a medal? Well these games are just like that, only better, because you won't cry and your parents won't tell you how proud they are of you even though it's obvious they're disappointed.

Get ready for the grand presentation by photocopying and enlarging the medals opposite.

Podium Aerobics

Three players (and one extra person)

Apparatus:

- 3 swivel chairs
- 3 buckets
- 10 one-pence pieces
- 10 two-pence pieces
- 10 five-pence pieces
- Bowl

Warm-up:

Adjust the swivel chairs so they are all different heights. Position them next to each other in the arrangement outlined in the diagram, with the three buckets in front of them. Fill the bowl with all of the coins and shake it up. Choose three players (perhaps the players who have performed strongest overall in other Office Olympics events) and label the buckets with their names. Nominate one non-player to be in charge of the bowl of money.

How to Play:

There's nothing like being awarded a nice shiny medal, but this game is all about competing for the top spot. All three players line up behind the middle chair (alphabetically by surname, for fairness' sake). With one minute on the clock, the person with the bowl of money must randomly grab a coin from the bowl and throw it to the first player in the line. If they catch it they must sit on the chair (podium) relevant to that coin (1 p = lowest podium; 2 p = middle podium; 5 p = highest podium) and throw it into their bucket. They then jump down and run to the back of the line. After one minute the player with the most money in their bucket is the winner and the three players should take their rightful places on the podiums according to the position they achieved.

Medal Hoopla

Two or more players (plus three willing colleagues)

Apparatus:

- 20 ten-pence pieces
- Ball of string
- Sticky tape

Warm-up:

To make the 20 medals tape each coin to a 60-cm length piece of string (see diagram). Place the medals in a pile at one end of the office. At the other end ask three colleagues to sit in a podium formation: one on the floor (bronze), one on a chair (silver) and one on a desk (gold).

How to Play:

Each player has three minutes to present their colleagues with as many medals as possible. Starting at the pile of medals, the player must grab one and sprint to the podium where they choose which colleague to present it to before performing the required forfeit.

- Bronze medal winner = no forfeit, return immediately to the pile of medals.
- Silver medal winner = perform five star jumps before returning to the pile of medals.
- Gold medal winner = perform five press-ups before returning to the pile of medals.

After the three minutes is up points are awarded for the number of medals worn by each colleague.

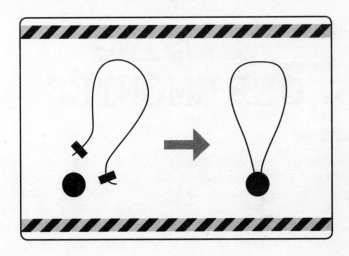

Scoring:

- 10 points are scored for every gold medal
- 5 points are scored for every silver medal
- 2 points are scored for every bronze medal

CLOSING CEREMONIES

The competition may be over, but it's not time to blow out the flame and sweep up the foam fingers just yet. No epic sports event is complete without a lavish closing ceremony, and neither are the Office Olympics. After proving yourself as worthy competitors, it's now time to prove you know how to celebrate. Here are a few ideas for how to bring your Office Olympics to an end in style.

- Proudly display your medals round your neck and wave your homemade flags as you parade around the office and walk ceremoniously to the pub to toast your success.

- Send out a group email to the company commending all the competitors for their efforts – maybe even set up a Facebook group and post some pictures of people taking part.

- Medals or not, everyone got involved and for their enthusiasm and commitment to office morale surely they deserve the afternoon off?

- Organise an office field trip (or lunch break) to a nearby park for a celebratory picnic – running shoes optional.

- Have a casual Friday where everyone must come to work in sports clothes – sweat bands mandatory.

- With your boss's permission (or your own permission if you're the head honcho), order in pizzas for Friday lunchtime. You're going to need that cheese after all the running around you've been doing.

- Have a Grecian-themed office party with special prizes for the most successful Office Olympians. Prizes could include a gold-sprayed stapler, a giant pencil, or a voucher for cups of tea.

OUTRAGEOUS OFFICE DARES

Suzie Duncan

ISBN: 978-1-84024-775-6

£5.99

Paperback

369 outrageous dares to help release your inner delinquent!

If you need some wicked inspiration for staving off office boredom:

- Discreetly lean over and sniff a colleague's armpit
- Applaud uproariously whenever someone comes out of the toilet
- Arrive late to a meeting and moonwalk to your seat

Do you dare to play?

F IN EXAMS

The Best Test Paper Blunders

Richard Benson

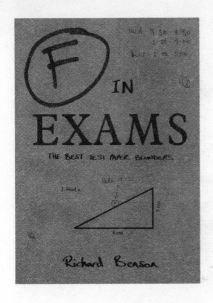

ISBN: 978-1-84024-700-8

£5.99

Paperback

We've all been there. You've been studying hard, the day of the BIG test arrives, you turn over the paper, and 'what the *&%@ does that mean?!' Not a clue.

This book is packed full of hilarious examples of the more creative ways that students have tackled those particularly awkward exam questions.

What happens during puberty to a boy?

He says goodbye to his childhood and enters adultery.

Explain the term 'free press'.

When your mum irons your trousers for you.

www.summersdale.com